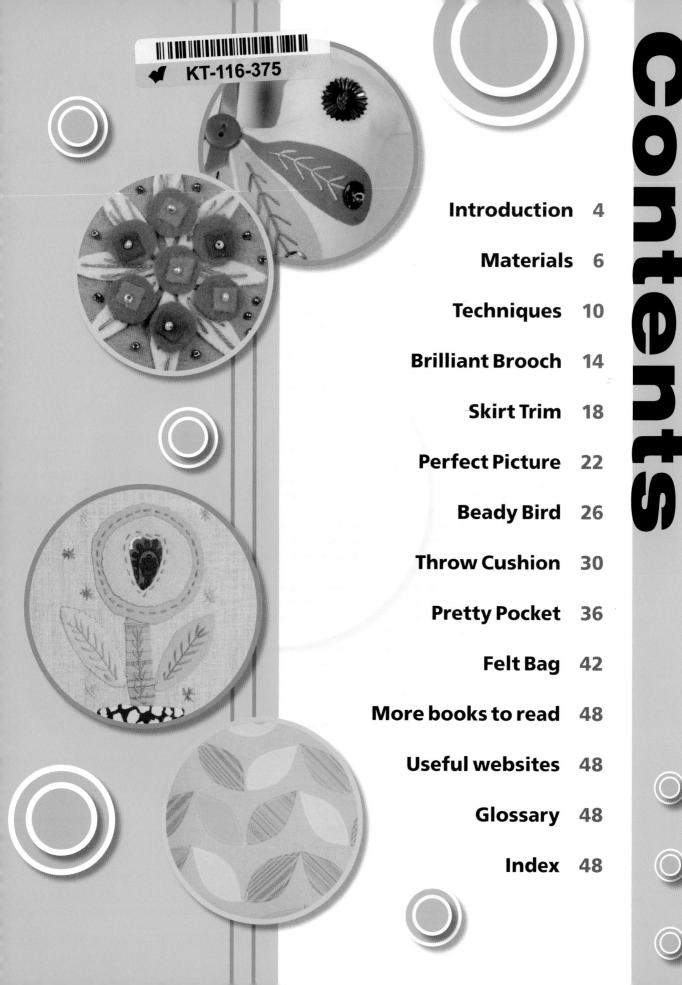

Contents

Introduction

FUNKY FACT

Appliqué is a great way to reuse old scraps of fabric. Start making a collection today!

Appliqué means to apply one smaller piece of fabric or decorative element to a background of fabric. When you wear out your jeans, and stitch a patch over the tear, this is appliqué!

Appliqué has been used throughout history to decorate clothes and home furnishings in countries all around the world. Whenever fabric was scarce, pieces of fabric were cut from old materials and sewn on to newer cloth to decorate it. Perhaps the earliest example is an Egyptian canopy of appliquéd leather dating from 980 BC. The best known use of appliqué is in the quilts produced from the 1600s to the present day in the USA and Europe. Visit museums and craft galleries to see appliqué from around the world.

Appliqué offers a wide range of creative possibilities and is used by many textile artists today. You can find clothing and household items decorated with appliqué and embroidery in many stores, and it is well worth looking around for ideas to try.

My very first introduction to sewing was sitting next to my mother watching her making dolls clothes for me. When I was old enough, she would give me scraps of material and beads and thread to experiment on my own.

I came to appliqué when my children were very small. The first items I made were little bibs, with animals and birds on them. I progressed to making quilts and wanted to add a very individual touch to the plain, bright colours I was using. So after designing some simple animal and bird shapes I applied them to the patchwork squares, making them very much more personal. I then began making appliquéd pictures using unusual fabrics, and layered pieces using silks and velvets, and covered in layers of hand and machine embroidery. I am continuously finding new and exciting ways to use appliqué in the projects I design, and just love the seemingly endless possibilities!

In this book you will find lots of easy projects, and once you have mastered the basic techniques, you will be able to start inventing other uses for this versatile craft. Many of the projects in the book can be made to give as a special handmade gift, to friends or family.

Materials

Fabrics

The best fabrics to use are crisp cottons. They come in various weights, from dress fabrics to heavier furnishing cottons, which are useful for cushion backs and bags. There are companies who sell 'fat quarters' for patchworkers. These are usually 45.7 x 56cm (18 x 22in), and are ideal for appliqué in both size and weight and not too expensive.

You will also need some bright pieces of felt for the Brilliant Brooch project on page 14.

I have listed some websites on page 48 that sell fabric online. You can of course use leftover scraps of fabric for appliqué, but make sure you choose colours and patterns that look good together for your projects.

Bias binding

This comes in many colours and is used in this book for a quick and simple edging for the Felt Bag project shown on page 42.

Felt is used in some of the projects.

A selection of crisp cotton fabrics and bias binding in several colours.

Sewing equipment

Sewing machine You do not need to have a very elaborate sewing machine. As long as yours does straight stitch and zigzag, you will have all you need to make the projects in the book.

Needles You will need a pack of various sewing needles and a beading needle, which has a very fine eye so that you can be sure it will fit through the hole in the bead.

Pins Glass-headed pins or ordinary sewing pins are fine.

Scissors You will need some sharp sewing scissors for cutting out fabric, and a pair of smaller sharp scissors for snipping threads and more intricate cutting.

Stranded embroidery threads There are some beautiful <u>stranded embroidery threads</u> on the market, in a rainbow of colours. It is a good idea to buy a selection of colours so that you have a variety to suit whichever project you are doing. The good thing about stranded threads is that you can choose the number of strands for the thickness you need.

Sewing threads You will also need a range of coloured sewing threads to use in your sewing machine. Some projects need the machine stitching to match the colour fabric you have chosen. You will also need ordinary sewing thread for tacking.

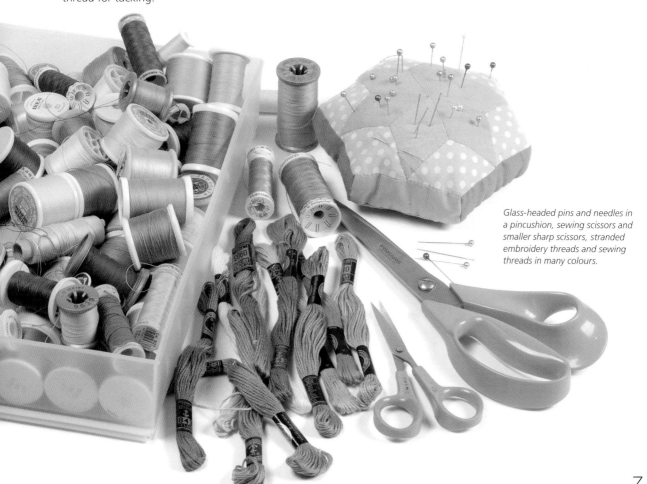

Glass-headed pins and needles in a pincushion, sewing scissors and smaller sharp scissors, stranded embroidery threads and sewing threads in many colours.

Embellishments

Beads You will need a selection of seed beads which you can buy in a wonderful array of colours. You may want to buy some slightly bigger beads too, if you think they will suit your project.

Sequins These can be bought in a great variety of shapes, sizes and colours in craft or fabric stores.

Buttons You can buy a selection of buttons at good fabric stores, or ask your friends and family if they have a 'button box' for odd buttons.

Ribbons You will need fine satin and organza ribbon for the projects in this book, from 3–5mm (⅛–¼in) wide. Choose ribbons to complement the colour of your chosen fabrics.

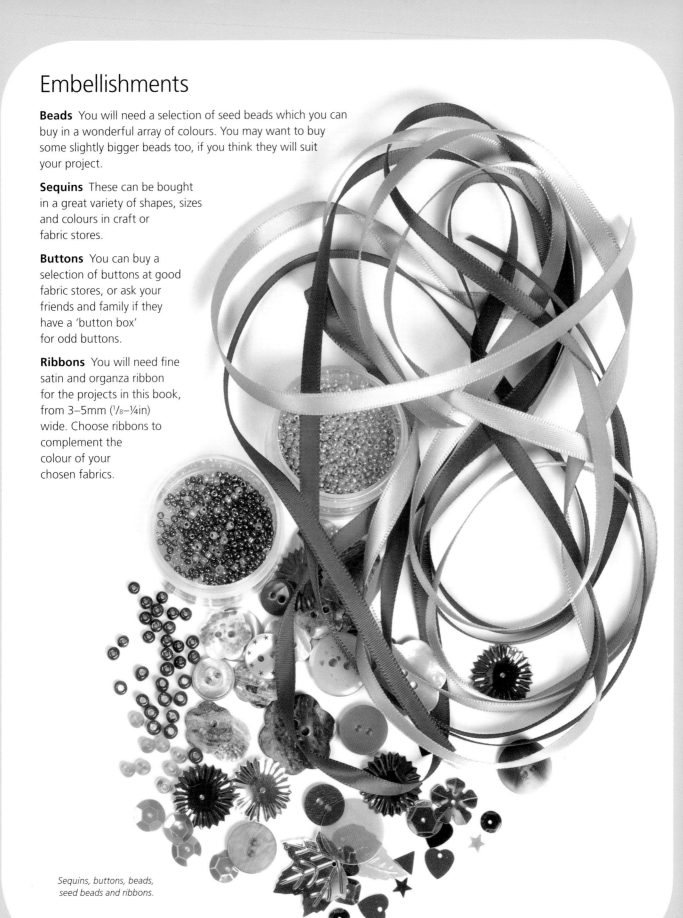

Sequins, buttons, beads, seed beads and ribbons.

Other materials

Fusible web This is a fine webbing of heat-activated material with a paper backing, used to fuse together two pieces of fabric. The paper side of the webbing is ironed to the reverse of the fabric. Then the template is drawn around and the shape cut out. After removing the backing paper the shape can be positioned and ironed into place.

Iron You will need an iron set to medium to hot when you are using fusible web. Always make sure you have an adult around when using a hot iron.

Kapok filling You will need to buy a bag of kapok filling or other stuffing from a craft or fabric store.

Ballpoint pen You will need a ballpoint pen and soft pencil for drawing around your patterns on to card.

Press studs These are known as 'snaps' in the USA. They are needed for the Pretty Pocket project on page 36. They need to be 5mm (¼in) wide.

Card Cereal boxes are the best kind of card for making templates and they are used for most of the projects in the book. Start collecting them and keep them handy.

Brown paper Ordinary brown packaging paper is useful for large patterns.

Brooch back You will need this to make the Brilliant Brooch project on page 14.

Cushion pad This is known as a 'pillow form' in the USA. You will need a 36 x 36cm (14¼ x 14¼in) cushion pad for the Throw Cushion project on page 30.

Techniques

Using fusible web

This is an easy way to attach the appliqué shapes to your background, ensuring that they are held in place while you apply decorative stitches, either by machine or hand sewing.

1 Place the fusible web sticky side down on the fabric and iron it on a hot setting.

2 Draw round your template with a pencil.

3 Cut out the shape.

4 Peel the backing paper off the fusible web.

5 Put the shape sticky side down on the backing fabric and iron it on using a hot setting.

The shape will now be firmly fixed on to your backing fabric.

Machine stitching

You can use a sewing machine to sew a seam, as shown below. You can also use it to sew on shapes instead of using fusible web or hand stitching.

1 Line up your fabric carefully. Use the gauge to set a 1cm (³/₈in) <u>seam allowance</u> and lower the machine's foot.

2 Set the machine to the stitch you want. This is running stitch. Press the foot pedal to sew.

3 When you have finished sewing, lift up the foot, slide out the sewn fabric and snip the threads.

Hand stitching

Starting and finishing running stitch

1 Thread your needle. Knot the end of the thread and bring the needle up from the back to the front of the fabric.

2 Take the needle down and then up and down again to make two evenly sized stitches.

3 Pull the thread through. Now you can see the stitches.

4 Continue sewing to make a row of stitches.

5 You now need to fasten off the stitching. At the back of the fabric, take the needle through the last stitch you made from right to left. Pull the thread through and repeat.

6 Take the needle through from right to left again, but do not pull it tight, leave a loop and take the needle through the loop.

7 Pull the thread through to make a knot and trim with scissors.

A finished row of running stitch.

TOP TiP!

Fasten off all your stitching in this way, not just running stitch.

Slip stitch appliqué

1 Thread the needle, knot the end and come up from the back of the backing fabric. Go through the edge of the shape.

2 Pull through and stitch through the backing fabric and the edge of the shape again.

3 Continue stitching right round the shape and fasten off at the back in the same way as for running stitch.

The finished appliquéd shape.

Closed fly stitch

  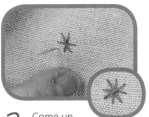 

1 Thread the needle and knot the end. Come up from the back and go down to make the first stitch, which is a kind of stalk. Bring the needle up again diagonally to the left.

2 Pull through. You can now see the stalk stitch. Make a loop round to the right and hold it down with your thumb. Go down to the top right of the stalk and bring the needle up at the bottom of the stalk. Pull through to reveal the stitch.

3 Come up at the top of the next stalk stitch to continue. When you have finished stitching, go down at the end and fasten off as before.

A finished row of closed fly stitch.

Star stitch

  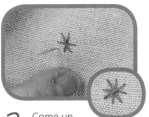 

1 Knot the end, come up from the back, make a straight stitch and go down.

2 Pull through. Find the middle of the first stitch. Come up to one side of it and go down on the other side to complete a cross shape.

3 Come up between the two bars of the cross to make a diagonal stitch across it. Come up again to start another diagonal stitch, and go down on the other side of the cross to complete the star shape.

Finished star stitches.

Sewing on beads

1 Use a fine needle that will go through the bead's hole. Come up from the back. Pick up a bead on your needle and push it to the bottom of the thread.

2 Go down close to where you came up and come up ready to sew on the next bead.

3 Pick up another bead and continue as before.

A row of beads.

Sewing on sequins with beads

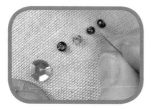

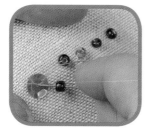

2 Pick up a bead as well, then go down through the same hole in the centre of the sequin. The bead will trap your sequin in place. When you have finished attaching sequins, fasten off at the back.

1 Knot the thread, come up from the back and pick up a sequin on your needle.

A row of sequins and beads.

Sewing on buttons

1 Thread the needle with doubled thread and knot the end. Come up through one of the central holes in the button and go down through the other one.

2 Repeat four times and fasten off at the back.

Ladder stitch

1 To sew up a gap in a piece, come up through the machine stitching to hide the knot inside the piece. Make a small stitch along the fold on one side of the gap.

2 Pull through and make another small stitch along the fold on the other side of the gap.

3 Continue until the whole gap is sewn up. To fasten off, go back under the machine stitching and up again.

4 Repeat several times and trim.

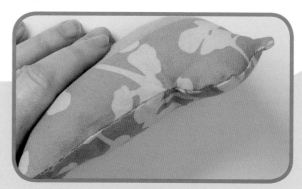

The finished stitching is very hard to see.

Brilliant Brooch

This brooch is made using brightly coloured felt and sparkling seed beads, and it would make any plain coat look individual and unusual. Try making brooches in different shapes and design your own motifs.

Patterns

The patterns for the brooch and its appliqué decorations, shown full size.

STAY SAFE

Always have an adult with you when you are ironing.

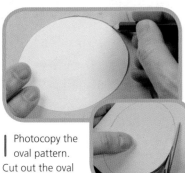

1 Photocopy the oval pattern. Cut out the oval shape and draw round it on a piece of card. Cut out the card oval to make a template.

2 Apply fusible web to pale blue and bright pink scraps of felt (see page 10). Make leaf and circle templates. Draw round the circle seven times on the fusible web on the bright pink felt. Draw round the leaf template eight times on the fusible web on the pale blue felt.

3 Apply fusible web to deep pink and orange felt scraps. Cut the scraps into strips 6mm (¼in) wide. Peel off the backing of the fusible web and cut the strips into three deep pink and four orange squares.

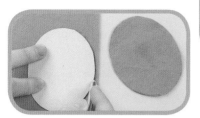

4 Make a template from the larger oval pattern, draw round it on green felt and cut out two oval shapes.

5 Peel off the backing from the pale blue felt leaves. Arrange the leaves in a circle, starting at the centre of one of the green felt ovals. Iron them on.

6 Thread a needle with one strand of bright pink embroidery thread. Knot the end. Make one long stitch in the centre of a leaf, then come up to the left of it. Go down at the base of the first central stitch, and come up to the right of it to make a second diagonal stitch.

TOP TIP!

When ironing on using fusible web, make sure the glue side is down.

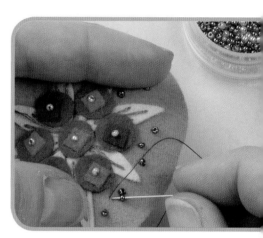

7 Peel off the backing from the circles. Place them in the centre of the brooch with the squares on top as shown. Iron them on, pressing firmly.

8 Thread a beading needle or fine-eyed needle with pink thread and knot the end. Come up through the centre of the square, pick up a green bead and go back down.

9 Complete all the squares, then sew three pink beads in each of the gaps between the leaves.

TOP TIP!

Keep seed beads in a saucer or little dish when you are sewing them on, to stop them rolling away.

10 Thread a needle and sew round the edge of each oval in long running stitches, 4mm (³⁄₁₆in) from the edge. Do not trim the tail of the thread.

11 Make two card templates from the smaller oval pattern. Put kapok filling in the decorated felt oval.

12 Put one small oval template on top of the kapok filling. Pull the tail of thread from the running stitches to gather the edges of the oval. With the thread pulled tight, make several stitches to secure the gathering.

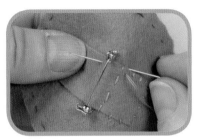

13 Cut a 1.5cm x 3cm (⁵⁄₈ x 1¼in) piece of the same green felt. Attach fusible web to it as shown on page 10 and peel off the backing. Thread the piece fusible web side down through the brooch back and iron it on to the second felt oval.

14 Thread a needle with doubled green thread and use straight stitches to sew the felt rectangle on to the oval to secure the brooch back.

15 Place the second small oval template in the centre of the felt oval on the other side from the brooch back. Pull the thread to gather the edges and secure with stitches as in step 12.

16 Thread a needle with two strands of embroidery thread and knot the end. Bring the needle up to hide the knot under the felt overlap of the decorated oval as shown.

17 Place the two ovals wrong sides together and sew them together using ladder stitch as shown on page 13.

What next?

Try using different colour schemes, motifs and decorative stitches to brighten up your brooches. They make great gifts for family and friends!

Skirt Trim

All through the centuries people have used appliqué to decorate their clothes, using ribbons, buttons and all manner of fabrics. Here is a way to decorate any piece of clothing, but it looks especially good on a flowing skirt. Once you have done this simple project, try making the design a little more elaborate by adding more flowers.

The circle pattern for the flowers, shown full size.

The arch pattern for the Skirt Trim, shown full size.

Patterns

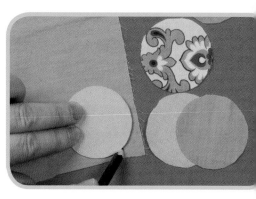

2 Make a card template from the circle in the same way. Draw round the template on your fabric scraps and cut out the circles.

1 Photocopy the arch pattern. Cut out the shape and draw round it on a piece of card. Cut out the card shape to make a template. Make the two little marks in the sides. Place the flat edge of the card template along the hem of your chosen skirt. Draw round the rounded part of the shape up to the little marks. Repeat all round the skirt.

3 Use your fingers to make a pleat in one of the fabric circles.

4 Thread a needle and make a couple of stitches in the centre of the circle to hold the pleat in place.

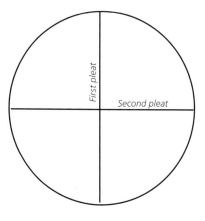

First pleat

Second pleat

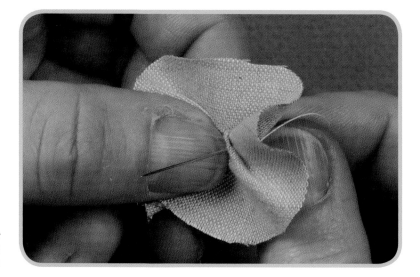

5 Turn the circle round and make the second pleat. Stitch it in place and fasten off securely.

6 Cut the organza ribbon into lengths of 21cm (8¼in). Place one length over one of your pencil lines, making sure the line is in the centre of the ribbon. Pin the ribbon in place.

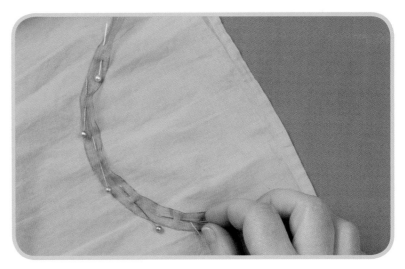

TOP TIP!

Always pin and tack your work first to make the final sewing easier.

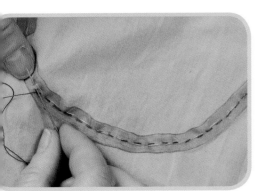

7 Tack the ribbon in place with long running stitches. Use contrasting thread to running stitch round the semi-circle. Here I have used red embroidery thread. Do not trim the thread at the end of the semi-circle.

8 Place a flower and a button on the end of the semi-circle of ribbon and use the tail end of the thread to sew them on as shown.

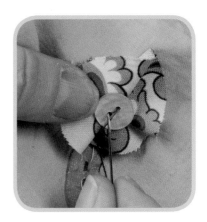

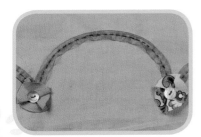

The finished skirt hem.

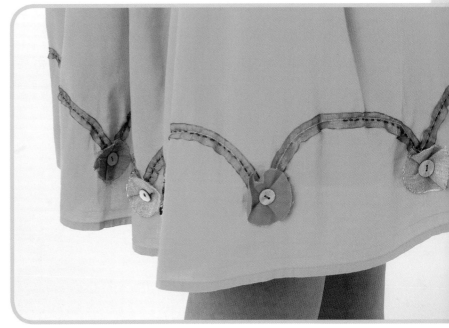

What next?

Try sewing flowers on to your jeans. You can make the flowers bigger or use several layers. It also looks good if you cut out the flowers with pinking shears.

Perfect Picture

You will need

Card, pencil and scissors

Scraps of seven different fabrics

Matching/contrasting sewing threads and embroidery threads

Needle and pins

Backing fabric, 14 x 21cm (5½ x 8¼in)

Iron

Button

Hand appliqué can be used in many different ways to make pictures like this one or unique cards and gifts. You can use the same technique to apply fabric to clothes, quilts or cushions. Once you have made this simple picture, you will be able to create your own designs.

The patterns for the Perfect Picture, shown full size. You will need to make card templates for the larger and the smaller shapes.

Patterns

1 Make a card template from the larger leaf pattern and draw round it on a scrap of purple fabric.

2 Cut out the leaf shape.

3 Thread a needle and sew round the shape 4mm ($^3/_{16}$in) from the edge, in running stitch. Do not trim the end as you are going to use it for gathering.

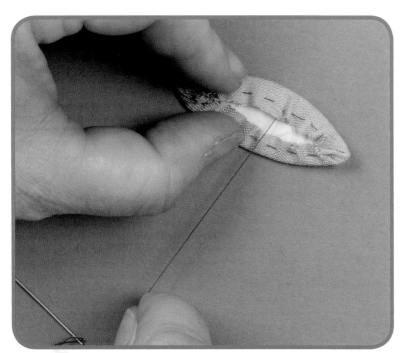

4 Make a card template from the smaller leaf shape. Place this in the centre of the fabric leaf and pull the tail of the thread to gather the edges.

5 Iron both sides of the leaf shape.

6 Do a couple of stitches to secure the gathering thread, then trim it. Take out the card template. Follow steps 1 to 6 for all the other shapes: the two flower circles and the heart, the flower pot and stalk and the other leaf. Use a variety of fabrics as shown.

7 Pin all the pieces in place on your backing fabric.

8 Slip stitch all the pieces in place (see page 11). Use matching thread for each piece.

TOP TIP!

When sewing shapes on to backing fabric, do not pull the stitches too tight.

9 Decorate the leaves with closed fly stitch as shown on page 12. Sew round the flower and the heart with running stitch and decorate the background with star stitch (see page 12). Sew a button on the flower pot (see page 13).

The finished picture in a frame.

What next?

Any simple drawing can be used for an appliqué picture. The fabric and stitching will create the detail, so the simpler the design the better!

25

Beady Bird

Appliquéd stuffed toys and hanging decorations have been made for hundreds of years. This bird is simple to make and once you have mastered one, you could make a whole family of them, all decorated in different ways. They make lovely Christmas decorations, or can be filled with lavender to make a sweet-smelling gift.

You will need

Card, pencil and scissors

Cream backing fabric

Fabric scraps in five plain colours, and fusible web to cover

Iron

Six sequins and six beads

Embroidery threads to contrast with fabrics

Pins and thread for tacking

Sewing machine with cream sewing thread

Kapok filling

Ribbon, 24cm (9½in) and button

Patterns

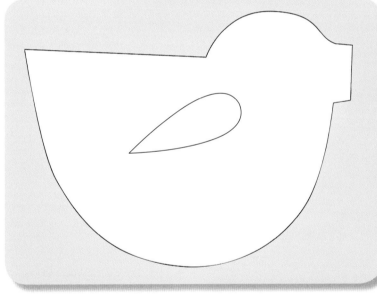

The patterns for the bird and the petal shape, shown half size. Enlarge them to 200% on a photocopier, then make card templates of them.

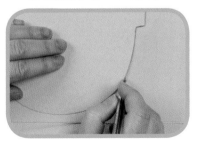

1 Enlarge the patterns on a photocopier and cut out the bird. Draw round it on card to make a template. Draw round the template on your backing fabric.

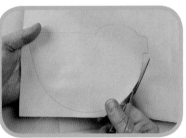

2 Cut out the shape. Repeat to make the other side of the bird.

3 Apply fusible web to the five fabric scraps. Make a card petal template and draw round it on the paper backing. You need one petal in each colour.

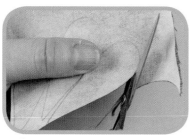

4 Cut out the shapes and peel off the backing.

5 Arrange the pieces on the bird shape and iron them on.

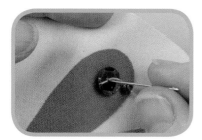

6 Sew a sequin and a bead on to the rounded edge of each petal shape as shown on page 13.

7 Choose a contrasting thread for each petal. Start at the sequin end and do closed fly stitch down each petal as shown on page 12.

8 Place the bird pieces right sides together and pin them. Use sewing thread to tack round the edge with large running stitches. Start 2cm (¾in) from the tail end, go round the bird and leave a 5cm (2in) gap on the bird's back. Fasten off and snip the end.

9 Thread up the machine and bobbin with cream thread. Set the gauge for a 1cm (³/₈in) seam. Start 2cm (¾in) below the tail and sew to the tail corner. If you have a back stitch on your machine, do one here. With the needle down, lift up the foot.

10 Turn the fabric through 180°, put the foot down and go back over the sewing you have just done to begin sewing round the shape. Sew very slowly round the edge of the head, one stitch at a time. Keep to the 1cm (³/₈in) gauge all the time.

11 Sew to the end of your tacking stitches, leaving the 5cm (2in) gap as before. Lift the foot with the needle up and slide the fabric out. Snip off the loose ends. Take out the pins, then cut and gently pull out the tacking stitches.

12 To keep the shape of the bird later, snip into the corners as shown, but do not snip right up to the stitching.

13 Trim round the edges and cut across the tail as shown. Do not trim across the gap.

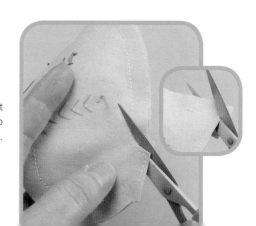

14 Trim diagonally across the flaps that are left across the gap. Do this at each end of the gap.

15 Fold back the flaps and press them with your fingers to make a sharp fold.

16 Thread a needle with sewing thread and sew each flap to its side of the bird, to tidy the flaps.

17 Turn the bird right sides out. Use blunt-ended, closed scissors to push out the beak shape and the tail.

18 Stuff the bird with the kapok filling. Start with the head and beak and finish with the tail, pushing in small lumps at a time. Do not overstuff the bird or you will stretch the seams.

19 Use cream sewing thread to sew up the gap using ladder stitch as shown on page 13. Take out the tacking stitches.

TOP TIP!

Push very gently when pushing out the shapes, or your scissors will go through the fabric.

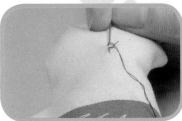

20 Make a few stitches where you want the bird's eye to be.

21 Sew on a sequin and a bead as shown on page 13. To finish, push the needle down through the sequin and up through the top of the head seam as shown. Snip off the thread close to the seam.

22 Place the ribbon as shown with both ends on the front of the bird. Sew through both ends and through both sides of the bird. Make four stitches and fasten off at the back. Use the same thread to sew on a button, as shown on page 13.

What next?

Try different shapes to decorate your bird, or use the hand appliqué method shown in the Perfect Picture project (page 22). You may want to try making other simple shapes to decorate and stuff.

Throw Cushion

You will need

Card, pencil and scissors

Four different fabric scraps, fusible web to cover, and iron

Cushion front fabric, 40 x 40cm (15¾ x 15¾in)

Cushion back fabric, two pieces, 40 x 26cm (15¾ x 10¼in) each

Sewing machine and threads to contrast with the fabrics and to match the back fabric

Needle and pins

Cushion pad (pillow form) 36 x 36cm (14¼ x 14¼in)

Decorate your bed with variations on this throw cushion design. They can either all have similar colours or be wildly different! Once you have mastered the machine appliqué technique, you could try inventing your own simple designs for throw cushions.

The patterns for the Throw Cushion, shown full size.

Patterns

Photocopy the patterns and cut them out. Draw round them on card and cut out card templates. Apply fusible web to your four fabrics (see page 10). Draw round the leaf templates six times on each of the four fabrics. Make three daisies from one fabric, and three circles from a contrasting fabric.

2 Peel the backing off all the shapes.

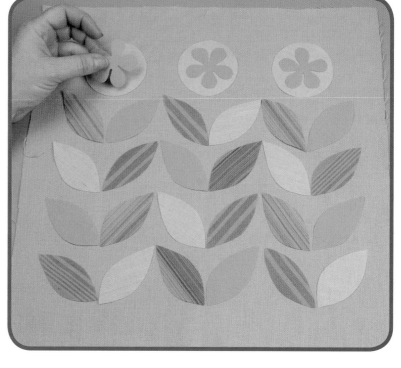

3 Lay out the throw cushion front fabric and arrange the pieces as shown, with the fusible web side down. Allow at least 3cm (1¼in) between the shapes and the edge of the fabric.

4 Iron the shapes on to the throw cushion front fabric.

STAY SAFE
Always have an adult with you when you are ironing.

5 Put contrasting thread in the sewing machine's bobbin. Sew carefully round the circles 3mm (¹/₈in) from the edge. To decorate the flowers, begin near the end of a petal and sew to the centre. Sew to near the end of the next petal, then leave the needle in, lift the foot and turn the fabric round. Sew back to the centre and move on to the next petal.

STAY SAFE
Always ask an adult to help you set up the sewing machine.

6 Turn up the long edge of one of the back fabric pieces 1cm (³/₈in) and iron the fold.

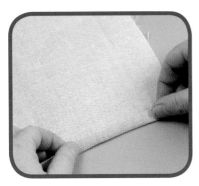

7 Fold the ironed edge over again and iron it again. Repeat steps 6 and 7 for the other back fabric piece.

8 Thread the sewing machine with matching sewing thread and sew just within the inner fold as shown. Repeat for the other back piece.

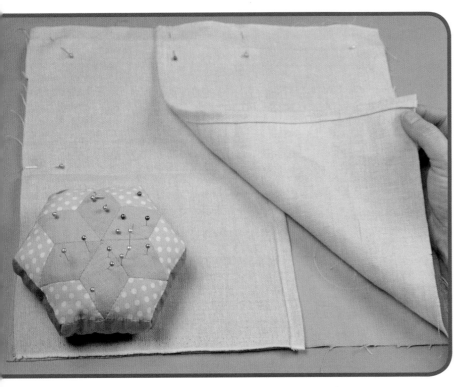

9 Pin the two back pieces to the wrong side of the front piece as shown.

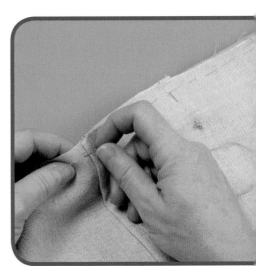

10 Tack the back pieces in place with long running stitches.

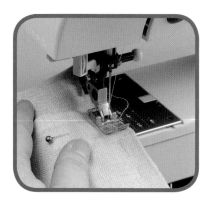 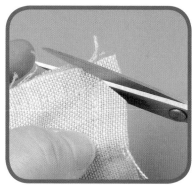 

11 Set the sewing machine's gauge for a 1cm (³/₈in) seam. Sew all the way round the edge of the throw cushion cover.

12 Remove the pins and the tacking. Snip across the corners, but do not cut as far as the stitching.

13 Turn the throw cushion cover right sides out. Push out the corners using blunt-ended, closed scissors. Now you can put in your cushion pad (pillow form).

The finished Throw Cushion.

What next?

Using the same templates, you can create many different designs. Try using only the flower motif on a really bright background for a flower power throw cushion!

Pretty Pocket

This desirable little pocket hangs from your belt and is a great way to keep your phone or wallet near you at all times. Hand appliqué and machine sewing are both used to make it. It is an old idea brought up to date, as pockets always used to be separate pieces of clothing attached to a belt.

You will need

Card, pencil and scissors

Main fabric and lining fabric, 21 x 28cm (8¼ x 11in) each

Five plain fabric scraps and one patterned

Sewing threads to match all fabrics

White embroidery thread

Needle and pins

Iron

Sewing machine

Press stud (snap)

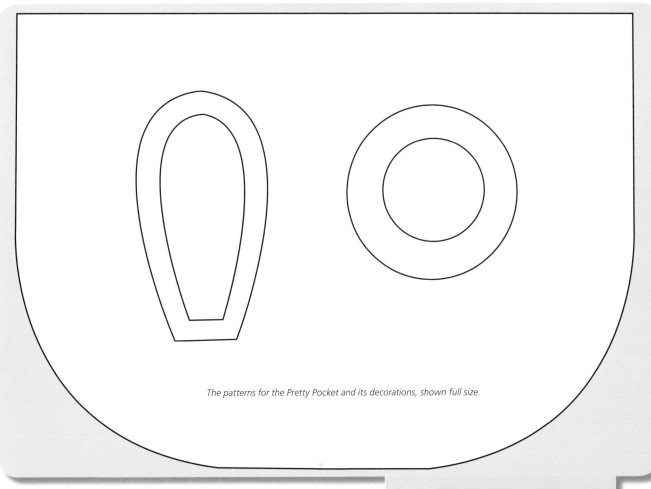

The patterns for the Pretty Pocket and its decorations, shown full size.

Patterns

I Photocopy the pattern for the Pretty Pocket and cut out the shape. Draw round the shape twice on your main fabric and twice on your lining fabric and cut out the pieces. Also cut out two 16 x 4cm (6¼ x 1½in) pieces from the main fabric and two from the lining fabric, to make the belt hooks.

2 Cut out the larger petal shape from the photocopy and draw round it on card to make a template. Draw round it on five different scraps of fabric.

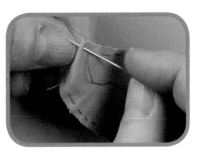

3 Thread a needle with sewing thread and sew in running stitch 3mm (1/8in) from the edge of a fabric petal. Do not trim the end of the thread.

4 Make a card template from the smaller petal shape and place it inside the fabric petal. Pull the tail of the thread to gather the edges.

5 Iron the petal flat, secure and trim the end of the thread, then take out the small template.

STAY SAFE

Always have an adult with you when you are ironing.

6 Make all the petals in the same way, then arrange them on the pocket shape and pin them in place. Sew each petal on using slip stitch (see page 11) in a matching sewing thread.

7 Use the larger circle pattern to cut out a circle from patterned fabric, then gather the edges around a card template made from the smaller circle pattern. Take out the template. Use slip stitch to sew on the circle in the centre of the petal design.

8 Use running stitch in white embroidery thread to sew round all the shapes.

37

9 To make a belt loop, place a main fabric piece and a lining piece right sides together. Set the sewing machine's gauge for a 1cm (³/₈in) seam allowance. Thread it with thread to match the main fabric. Start to sew near the middle of a long side. Do a back stitch, then change to straight stitch. Sew for a few centimetres (1in), then turn and go back in the other direction. When you come to a corner, lift the foot with the needle in, turn the piece, lower the foot and continue. Sew right round the shape but leave a 6cm (2³/₈in) gap in the long side where you started.

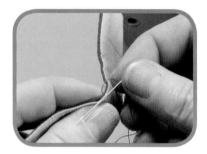

10 Snip off the corners and trim the edges so that the belt hook will be neater when it is turned right sides out. Make sure you do not cut up to the stitching.

11 Turn the belt hook right sides out and use closed, blunt scissors to push out the corners. Iron the belt hook flat.

12 Sew up the gap using ladder stitch (see page 13). Repeat steps 9–12 to make the second belt hook.

13 Place the embroidered bag front piece and a lining piece right sides together. Keeping to the 1cm (³/₈in) seam allowance, sew across the top flat edge.

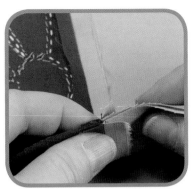

$|4$ Repeat step 13 to sew together the plain back piece and the other lining piece.

$|5$ Open the seams of the front and back pieces and iron them flat as shown.

$|6$ Place the front and back pieces right sides together and line up the seams as shown.

$|8$ Snip into all four curved edges, making sure you do not cut right up to the machine stitching.

$|7$ Pin the front and back pieces together. Sew round the piece with a 1cm (³/₈in) seam allowance, leaving a 6cm (2³/₈in) opening in the rounded part of the lining.

19 Turn the pocket right sides out and push out the seams using closed, blunt scissors.

20 Sew up the gap using ladder stitch (see page 13) and sewing thread to match the lining.

21 Push the lining inside the pocket and iron the pocket.

22 Fold the belt hooks in half and place the ends just inside the back of the pocket as shown. Pin them in place.

23 Machine sew the belt hooks in place, sewing back and forth across the ends several times.

24 Thread a needle with doubled sewing thread and knot the end. Sew on half of a press stud (snap) in the centre of the pocket back. Hide the knot under the press stud. Sew through the lining only, not right through to the back of the pocket. Sew the other half on to the lining inside the front of the pocket.

The finished Pretty Pocket.

What next?

Make this pocket in different colours to match your favourite outfits, or use other motifs from the book to decorate it.

Felt Bag

This simple appliquéd bag can be decorated as much or as little as you like, and uses up the scraps of fabric you may have left over from other projects. Try making it in colours to go with an outfit you love, or make a smaller version for a party. It would also make a lovely gift for a special friend.

You will need

Brown paper, pencil and scissors

Felt and lining fabric, ½m (19¾in) each

Fabric scraps and matching/contrasting sewing threads and embroidery threads

Fusible web and iron

Sewing machine

Needle, pins and buttons

Bias binding 1m (39½in)

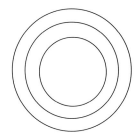

Patterns

The patterns for the Felt Bag and the designs on it, shown at half their actual size. You will need to enlarge them to 200 percent on a photocopier. The dotted line is the fold line at the bottom of the bag.

STAY SAFE

Always have an adult with you when you are ironing.

1 Enlarge the bag pattern to its full size on a photocopier and cut out the shape. Draw round it to make a card template. Fold your felt in half and place the template so that the bottom line (dotted in the pattern) is on the fold. Draw round the template and cut out the bag shape. Do the same on your lining fabric.

2 Apply fusible web to your fabric scraps as shown on page 10. Make card templates for the circles, leaf and stalks. Draw round the templates and cut out shapes as follows: one large and one medium circle; four small circles; nine leaves; one large stalk and four smaller stalks. Trim the ends of two of the smaller stalks to make them shorter still. Peel off the backing.

TOP TIP!

Go slowly when stitching down shapes using the sewing machine, especially with the circles.

3 Place all the shapes to create the design as shown and iron them on to the felt bag front.

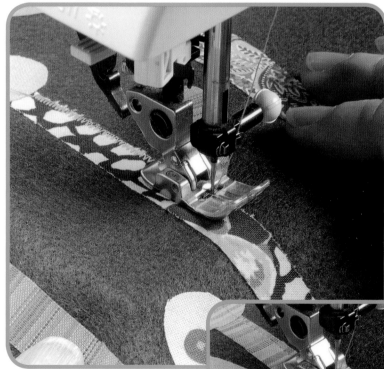

STAY SAFE

Always ask an adult to help you set up the sewing machine.

4 Machine sew round some of the shapes, using thread in two different colours chosen to match or contrast with your fabrics. Use straight stitch for some of the shapes and zigzag stitch for others.

5 Hand sew round some of the shapes in running stitch using two strands of embroidery thread. Sew round the outsides of some of the flowers and leaves in the same way using either bright or white threads.

6 Sew a button in the centre of each flower (see page 13).

7 Turn the felt bag inside out and use a sewing machine and matching sewing thread to sew up the side seams, leaving a 1cm (³/₈in) seam allowance.

8 Trim the corners, making sure you do not cut as far as the stitching.

9 Sew across the top of the handle in the same way. Now repeat steps 7–9 to sew up the lining.

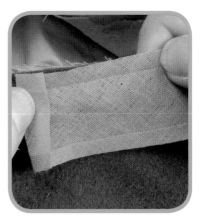

10 Put the lining in the bag, making sure you match up the seams of the lining with the seams of the bag.

11 Pin and tack the lining in place. Tack with large running stitches, 5mm (¼in) from the edge, round both the openings in the bag.

12 Take a length of bias binding and open up the fold on one side of it. Place it as shown just beyond the side seam of the felt bag. Fold over the end.

13 Pin the bias binding in place, following the curve of the bag's opening.

14 When you come back round to where you started, overlap the bias binding slightly, then trim the end. Tack the bias binding in place with long running stitches.

15 Machine sew the bias binding to the felt bag, leaving a 1cm (³/₈in) seam allowance. Sew slowly and carefully round the curves.

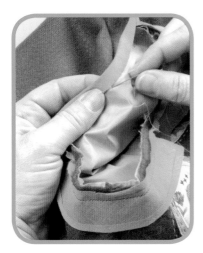

16 Fold the bias binding over the bag opening to hide the machine stitching. Slip stitch it in place (see page 11). Repeat steps 12–16 to complete the bag.

The finished bag.

What next?

Just by using different designs and colour ways you can adapt this simple bag to any style and taste. Try making a small one to take to a party!

47

More books to read

Appliqué by Lucinda Ganderton, Quadrille Publishing Ltd, 2006
Bend the Rules Sewing by Amy Karol, Potter Craft, 2007
The Complete Book of Patchwork, Quilting, and Appliqué by
Linda Seward, Mitchell Beazley, 1996
Craft Workshop: Appliqué by Petra Boase, Southwater, 2003
Easy Appliqué Samplers by Mimi Dietrich, Martingale
& Co., 2005
Quilting, Patchwork and Appliqué: A World Guide by Caroline
Crabtree and Christine Shaw, Thames and Hudson, 2007

Useful websites

www.cottonpatch.co.uk

www.thetabbycat.com

www.purlsoho.com

www.craft-felt.co.uk

www.quilterscloth.co.uk

www.calicolaine.co.uk

Glossary

Appliqué Cutting shapes from one fabric and applying them to the surface of another.

Seam allowance This is the distance between the cut edges of the fabric and the stitching when you sew two pieces of fabric together. You can set the gauge on your sewing machine for the seam allowance that you want.

Stranded embroidery thread This is a loosely twisted thread made up of six strands, used for hand embroidery techniques. The strands can be separated so that the thread can be as thick or as thin as you want it for your embroidery.

Index